# BRUCE GOLDSTONE

# SPECTACULAR SPRING

HENRY HOLT AND COMPANY

NEW YORK

SPRING
IS A
SEASON
OF
SPECTACULAR
BEGINNINGS.

Green plants and colorful flowers begin to grow.

Animals shake off the cold of winter.

People start spending more time outdoors.

# DAYS GET LONGER . . .

Spring begins on the vernal equinox. In the Northern Hemisphere, that's a day near March 20 when day and night are both 12 hours long.

# . . . AND NIGHTS GET SHORTER.

Spring ends on the summer solstice. In the Northern Hemisphere, that's a day near June 21. It's the longest day of the year.

# DAYS BEGIN TO GET WARMER . . .

At the start of spring, you might still wear a sweater, a scarf, and warm gloves.

# . . . SO YOUR CLOTHES GET LIGHTER.

As the days begin to get warmer, you won't need so many heavy layers. But you might put on a raincoat and boots. Waterproof clothing helps keep you dry when it rains.

# AND SPRING RAIN STARTS.

When the air gets warmer in
spring, it's more likely to rain than snow.
Air always holds tiny drops of water vapor, and
warm air holds more than cold air. As warm air rises, it
cools, and water droplets come together to form clouds.
When the droplets get too heavy to stay in the
cloud, they fall to the ground as rain.

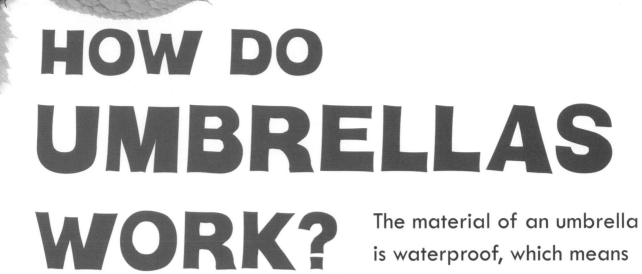

# HOW DO UMBRELLAS WORK?

The material of an umbrella is waterproof, which means rain will bounce off instead of passing through.

When you open the umbrella, thin ribs unfold and stretch out the material to form a dome. Many umbrellas have an automatic spring. When you press a button, the spring releases and the umbrella pops open.

Sometimes wind in a rainstorm will push up inside the umbrella. The ribs flip up and the umbrella turns inside out. You can usually tug the umbrella back into the right shape.

AFTER
THE RAIN,
YOU MIGHT SEE
A RAINBOW.

Sunlight is made up of many colors, but normally we can't see them all. After it rains, there are still a lot of water droplets in the air. When sunlight hits these droplets from a certain angle, the beam of light separates into the colors that are usually mixed together in sunlight. A beautiful rainbow is the result. The colors in a rainbow are always in the same order.

**RED**

**ORANGE**

**YELLOW**

**GREEN**

**BLUE**

**INDIGO**

**VIOLET**

fuzzy

# HOW DOES SPRING FEEL?

wet

velvety

soft

muddy

squishy

fluffy

windy

leafy

smooth

cherry tree

forsythia

grass

azalea

PLANTS START TO GROW ALL OVER THE PLACE.

dogwood tree

apple tree

magnolia tree

Spring rain brings water that plants need to start growing. Look around and you'll see leaves and flowers starting to grow on trees, on bushes, and on the ground.

rhododendron

# FLOWER BULBS BEGIN TO BLOOM.

hyacinth

tulip

bulb (this part is underground)

grape hyacinth

Many of the first flowers to bloom in spring grow from bulbs that have been in the ground all winter. Unlike seeds, bulbs do not have a hard outer layer. Instead, bulbs have many layers called scales that help the bulb survive in the cold. The same bulb can grow a new plant every spring.

allium

daffodil
(narcissus)

iris

snowdrops

crocus

# WHAT DOES SPRING SMELL LIKE?

Spring is a great time to close your eyes and sniff. Smells travel more easily in warm air than in cold air. As spring days get warmer, you'll find many fresh new smells when you walk outdoors.

# SPROUTS
## SPRING UP
### FROM SEEDS
# UNDERGROUND.

Spring rain also helps seeds begin to grow in a process called germination. Temperature, sunlight, and water need to be right for a seed to germinate.

First, the seed takes in water and swells. Then the outer layer, or seed coat, splits open. The plant's root grows downward and the baby stem grows upward.

A sprout is the first
part of the plant to
appear aboveground.
A seed can grow into
a new plant only once.

# SEEDS TRAVEL IN MANY WAYS.

Plants don't have legs, but they can still travel. Some seeds travel in the air. For example, dandelion seeds have a feathery part that helps the wind carry them to fresh new ground. The seeds of a maple tree have wings that make them move like helicopters through the air.

Other seeds are sticky or prickly. They catch a ride by traveling in animal fur or feathers—or on people's clothing. When they finally fall to the ground, they might grow where they land.

Seeds can travel by water, too. When plants that hang over water let go of their seeds, the current carries them along to new soil.

Animals can also move seeds. Birds like robins eat seeds, but they do not use the entire seed for energy. The seeds pass through the bird's digestive system and then get dropped out, along with some natural fertilizer that feeds the seeds.

# FARMERS PLANT NEW CROPS.

In spring, farmers plant seeds that will grow into crops like vegetables and grains. First, they prepare the soil. Then they plant, or sow, the seeds. Water and fertilizer help crops grow into strong plants.

Some seeds need to be sown by hand, but others are sown using farm machines called seeders.

These machines can dig soil and spread seeds evenly.

# WHAT SHAPE IS SPRING?

Look for shapes in spring. Some flower petals are shaped like raindrops.

What do you see that's round? What other shapes do you see?

Umbrellas often have eight sides
when you look at them from the top.
That shape is called an octagon.

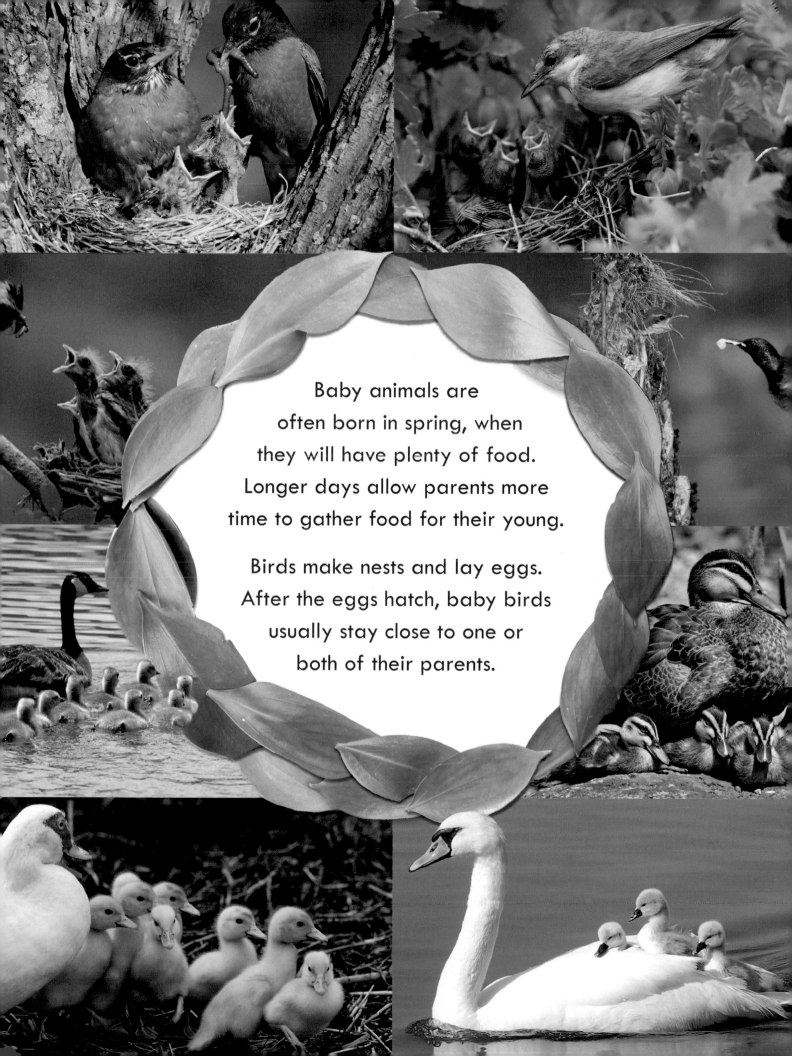

Baby animals are
often born in spring, when
they will have plenty of food.
Longer days allow parents more
time to gather food for their young.

Birds make nests and lay eggs.
After the eggs hatch, baby birds
usually stay close to one or
both of their parents.

# HOW DO BABY BIRDS HATCH?

Inside an egg, the yolk and the white provide food the baby needs to grow. When it's time to hatch, the baby bird uses its beak to knock a hole through the shell.

After hatching, birds usually stay in the nest near a parent as they grow. When their feathers and wings are ready to fly, baby birds become fledglings. Parents still help to care for fledglings until they can find food and protect themselves on their own.

WHAT DOES SPRING **SOUND** LIKE?

CHEEP

DRIP DROP

TWEET

PITTER-PATTER

CHIRP BAA

CRACK
BOOM

PEEP

WHOOSH
RUSTLE

SPLISH!

SPLASH!

SPLOSH!

# SOME ANIMALS GET MOVING.

Warm spring weather tells some animals it's time to wake up and move.

Animals like chipmunks, bats, bears, frogs, and toads that hibernate or sleep a lot during the winter can find more food in spring. They wake up and become more active.

Birds that flew south in autumn fly north in spring. They will feed on new plants and insects and find places to nest.

# LITTLE CRITTERS
## GET BUSY, TOO.

Bees and other insects start flying from flower to flower. While they gather food, they also help pollinate plants. They carry pollen from one flowering plant to another, allowing the plants to make seeds. Birds, bats, and the wind carry pollen, too.

When worms start looking for food, they also help plants. As they move, they loosen the earth, which makes it easier for plant roots to grow. Worms eat old plants and very small living things and then leave behind natural fertilizer that plants can use for energy.

Tadpoles hatch from eggs in ponds and lakes. As they get bigger, they begin to grow lungs and legs and lose their gills and tails. Then the little froglets can hop around on land and eventually become adult frogs.

# PEOPLE HAVE MANY WAYS TO CELEBRATE IN SPRING.

Easter

Passover

April Fools' Day

Earth Day

Mother's Day

Memorial Day

# FRESH SPRING AIR GETS PEOPLE TO OPEN WINDOWS AND CLEAN UP.

Warm spring weather means we can open windows and let in some air. Many people use this time to do some spring cleaning. They tidy up indoors and out. Fresh paint can brighten a fence, porch, or door. Volunteers pitch in to help clean public places.

Of course, sometimes we just open windows to enjoy a cool breeze.

WHEN ALL
THE YEAR'S
BEGINNINGS HAVE
BEGUN,

SPECTACULAR SPRING
TURNS INTO

SUPER
SUMMER.

# SOME SPECTACULAR SPRING ACTIVITIES

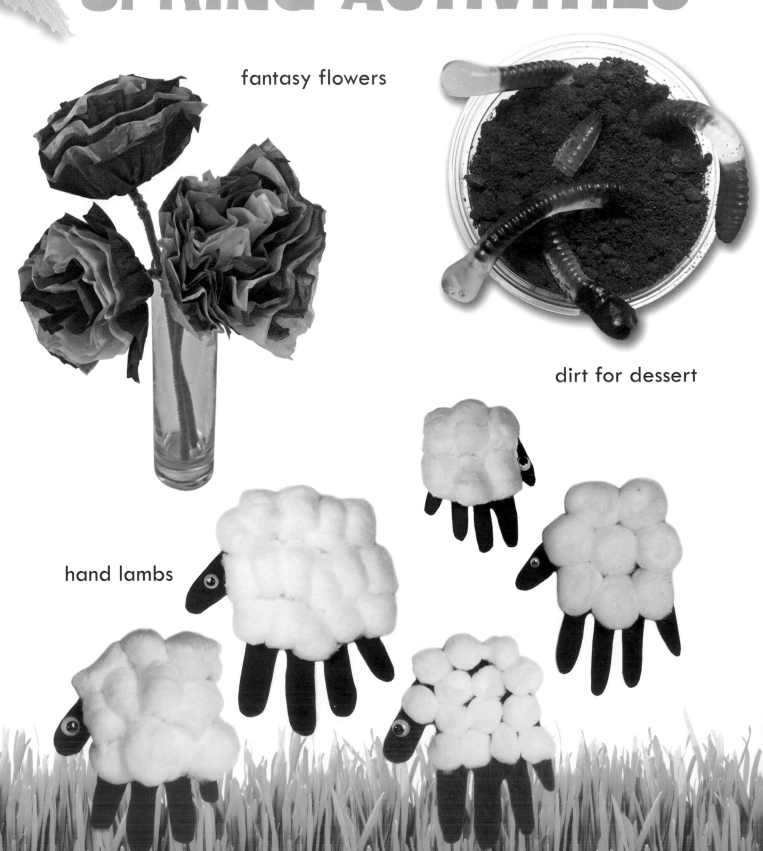

fantasy flowers

dirt for dessert

hand lambs

seed jars

mud painting

rain stick

**Turn the page for instructions.**

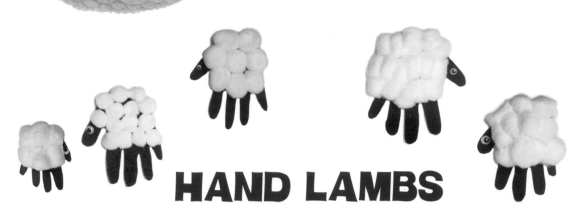

# HAND LAMBS

Trace your hand on black construction paper or felt. Cut out the hand (use safety scissors or ask an adult for help). Glue cotton balls or pom-poms to create the sheep's wool. Draw a face with white crayon or add googly eyes.

# RAIN STICK

Press thumbtacks, brads, or small nails into a cardboard tube. The more you use, the more sound your rain stick will make. Tape one end of the tube shut. Fill about a third of the tube with rice, beans, or other small objects. Tape the other end of the tube shut. Decorate your rain stick with colored tape, tissue paper, stickers, paint, or other art supplies. Tip the tube to hear the rain sound. To create a longer-lasting rain sound, use a longer, thicker cardboard tube, and ask an adult to help you hammer in plenty of nails.

# FANTASY FLOWERS

Start with five to seven squares of tissue paper, each about six inches wide. Stack the squares and accordion-fold them along one side. Twist a pipe cleaner around the center. Pull the paper layers away from the center one at a time to shape the flower. (You can also use newspaper or magazine paper squares. Crumple and uncrumple each square many times to make it softer and easier to work with.)

# DIRT FOR DESSERT

Twist open chocolate sandwich cookies and remove the cream fillings. Place the cookies in a plastic bag. Seal it and use a rolling pin or your hands to crush the cookies. Add chocolate pudding to a cup or mug. Top with cookie crumbs and add a few gummy worms. (You can also mix some cookie crumbs into the chocolate pudding to create a crunchy texture.)

# SEED JARS

Fill a glass jar with wet white paper towels. Use a pencil or your fingers to place seeds against the glass, one or two inches down from the top of the jar. Add more water as the towels dry out, but do not soak the seeds. Place on a sunny windowsill.

 # MUD PAINTING

Mix mud, water, a squirt of dishwashing liquid, and food coloring (or powdered tempera paint). Paint on thick cardboard or poster board (thin paper will wrinkle).

Thanks to Anna and Sophia Troetel, Chloe
and Charley London, and Jack Moeller for
their help with the jaunty hand lambs.

—B. G.

Henry Holt and Company, *Publishers since 1866*
Henry Holt® is a registered trademark of Macmillan Publishing Group, LLC
175 Fifth Avenue, New York, NY 10010 • mackids.com

Library of Congress Cataloging-in-Publication Data
Names: Goldstone, Bruce, author.
Title: Spectacular spring / Bruce Goldstone.
Description: First edition. | New York : Henry Holt and Company, 2018. |
Audience: Age 4–8.
Identifiers: LCCN 2017021145 | ISBN 9781250120144 (hardcover)
Subjects: LCSH: Spring—Juvenile literature. | Seasons—Juvenile literature.
Classification: LCC QB637.5 .G65 2018 | DDC 508.2—dc23
LC record available at https://lccn.loc.gov/2017021145

Our books may be purchased in bulk for promotional, educational, or business use.
Please contact your local bookseller or the Macmillan Corporate and Premium Sales Department
at (800) 221-7945 ext. 5442 or by e-mail at MacmillanSpecialMarkets@macmillan.com.

First edition, 2018 / Designed by Rebecca Syracuse
Photo collages created with images from shutterstock.com and Bruce Goldstone.
Printed in China by Toppan Leefung Printing Ltd.,
Dongguan City, Guangdong Province

1  3  5  7  9  10  8  6  4  2